Egyptian Precepts

Charles F. Horne

Precepts of the prefect, the lord Ptah-hotep, under the Majesty of the King of the South and North, Assa, living eternally forever.

The prefect, the feudal lord Ptah-hotep, says: O Ptah with the two crocodiles, my lord, the progress of age changes into senility. Decay falls upon man and decline takes the place of youth. A vexation weighs upon him every day; sight fails, the ear becomes deaf; his strength dissolves without ceasing. The mouth is silent, speech fails him; the mind decays, remembering not the day before. The whole body suffers. That which is good becomes evil; taste completely disappears. Old age makes a man altogether miserable; the nose is stopped up, breathing no more from exhaustion. Standing or sitting there is here a condition of . . . Who will cause me to have authority to speak, that I may declare to him the words of those who have heard the counsels of former days? And the counsels heard of the gods, who will give me authority to declare them? Cause that it be so and that evil be removed from those that are enlightened; send the double . . . The majesty of this god says: Instruct him in the sayings of former days. It is this which constitutes the merit of the children of the great. All that which makes the soul equal penetrates him who hears it, and that which it says produces no satiety.

Beginning of the arrangement of the good sayings, spoken by the noble lord, the divine father, beloved of Ptah, the son of the king, the first-born of his race, the prefect and feudal lord Ptah-hotep, so as to instruct the ignorant in the knowledge of the arguments of the good sayings. It is profitable for him who hears them, it is a loss to him who shall transgress them. He says to his son:

Be not arrogant because of that which you know; deal with the ignorant as with the learned; for the barriers of art are not closed, no artist being in possession of the perfection to which he should aspire. But good words are more difficult to find than the emerald, for it is by slaves that that is discovered among the rocks of pegmatite.

If you find a disputant while he is hot, and if he is superior to you in ability, lower the hands, bend the back, do not get into a passion with him. As he will not let you destroy his words, it is utterly wrong to interrupt him; that proclaims that you are incapable of keeping yourself calm, when you are contradicted. If then you have to do with a disputant while he is hot, imitate one who does not stir. You have the advantage over him if you keep silence when he is uttering evil words. "The better of the two is he who is impassive," say the bystanders, and you are right in the opinion of the great.

If you find a disputant while he is hot, do not despise him because you are not of the same opinion. Be not angry against him when he is wrong; away with such a thing. He fights against himself; require him not further to flatter your feelings. Do not amuse yourself with the spectacle which you have before you; it is odious, it is mean, it is the part of a despicable soul so to do. As soon as you let yourself be moved by your feelings, combat this desire as a thing that is reproved by the great.

If you have, as leader, to decide on the conduct of a great number of men, seek the most perfect manner of doing so that your own conduct may be without reproach. Justice is great, invariable, and assured; it has not been disturbed since the age of Ptah. To throw obstacles in the way of the laws is to open the way before violence. Shall that which is below gain the upper hand, if the unjust does not attain to the place of justice? Even he who says: I take for myself, of my own free-will; but says not: I take by virtue of my authority. The limitations of justice are invariable; such is the instruction which every man receives from his father.

Inspire not men with fear, else Ptah will fight against you in the same manner. If any one asserts that he lives by such means, Ptah will take away the bread from his mouth; if any one asserts that he enriches himself thereby, Ptah says: I may take those riches to myself. If any one asserts that he beats others, Ptah will end by reducing him to impotence. Let no one inspire men with fear; this is the will of Ptah. Let one provide sustenance for them in the lap of peace; it will then be that they will freely give what has been torn from them by terror.

If you are among the persons seated at meat in the house of a greater man than yourself, take that which he gives you, bowing to the ground. Regard that which is placed before you, but point not at it; regard it not frequently; he is a blameworthy person who departs from this rule. Speak not to the great man more than he requires, for one knows not what may be displeasing to him. Speak when he invites you and your worth will be pleasing. As for the great man who has plenty of means of existence, his conduct is as he himself wishes. He does that which pleases him; if he desires to repose, he realizes his intention. The great man stretching forth his hand does that to which other men do not attain. But as the means of existence are under the will of Ptah, one can not rebel against it.

If you are one of those who bring the messages of one great man to another, conform yourself exactly to that wherewith he has charged you; perform for him the commission as he has enjoined you. Beware of altering in speaking the offensive words which one great person addresses to another; he who perverts the trustfulness of his way, in order to repeat only what produces pleasure in the words of every man, great or small, is a detestable person.

If you are a farmer, gather the crops in the field which the great Ptah has given you, do not boast in the house of your neighbors; it is better to make oneself dreaded by one's deeds. As for him who, master of his own way of acting, being all-powerful, seizes the goods of others like a crocodile in the midst even of watchment, his children are an object of malediction, of scorn, and of hatred on account of it, while his father is grievously distressed, and as for the mother who has borne him, happy is another rather than herself. But a man becomes a god when he is chief of a tribe which has confidence in following him.

If you abase yourself in obeying a superior, your conduct is entirely good before Ptah. Knowing who you ought to obey and who you ought to command, do not lift up your heart against him. As you know that in him is authority, be respectful toward him as belonging to him. Wealth comes only at Ptah's own goodwill, and his caprice only is the law; as for him who . . Ptah, who has created his superiority, turns himself from him and he is overthrown.

Be active during the time of your existence, do no more than is commanded. Do not spoil the time of your activity; he is a blameworthy person who makes a bad use of his moments. Do not lose the daily opportunity of increasing that which your house possesses. Activity produces riches, and riches do not endure when it slackens.

If you are a wise man, bring up a son who shall be pleasing to Ptah. If he conforms his conduct to your way and occupies himself with your affairs as is right, do to him all the good you can; he is your son, a person attached to you whom your own self has begotten. Separate not your heart from him.... But if he conducts himself ill and transgresses your wish, if he rejects all counsel, if his mouth goes according to the evil word, strike him on the mouth in return. Give orders without hesitation to those who do wrong, to him whose temper is turbulent; and he will not deviate from the straight path, and there will be no obstacle to interrupt the way.

If you are employed in the larit, stand or sit rather than walk about. Lay down rules for yourself from the first: not to absent yourself even when weariness overtakes you. Keep an eye on him who enters announcing that what he asks is secret; what is entrusted to you is above appreciation, and all contrary argument is a matter to be rejected. He is a god who penetrates into a place where no relaxation of the rules is made for the privileged.

If you are with people who display for you an extreme affection, saying: "Aspiration of my heart, aspiration of my heart, where there is no remedy! That which is said in your heart, let it be realized by springing up spontaneously. Sovereign master, I give myself to your opinion. Your name is approved without speaking. Your body is full of vigor, your face is above your neighbors." If then you are accustomed to this excess of flattery, and there be an obstacle to you in your desires, then your impulse is to obey your passion. But he who . . . according to his caprice, his soul is . . ., his body is . . . While the man who is master of his soul is superior to those whom Ptah has loaded with his gifts; the man who obeys his passion is under the power of his wife.

Declare your line of conduct without reticence; give your opinion in the council of your lord; while there are people who turn back upon their own words when they speak, so as not to offend him who has put forward a statement, and answer not in this fashion: "He is the great man who will recognize the error of another; and when he shall raise his voice to oppose the other about it he will keep silence after what I have said."

If you are a leader, setting forward your plans according to that which you decide, perform perfect actions which posterity may remember, without letting the words prevail with you which multiply flattery, which excite pride and produce vanity.

If you are a leader of peace, listen to the discourse of the petitioner. Be not abrupt with him; that would trouble him. Say not to him: "You have already recounted this." Indulgence will encourage him to accomplish the object of his coming. As for being abrupt with the complainant because he described what passed when the injury was done, instead of complaining of the injury itself let it not be! The way to obtain a clear explanation is to listen with kindness.

If you desire to excite respect within the house you enter, for example the house of a superior, a friend, or any person of consideration, in short everywhere where you enter, keep yourself from making advances to a woman, for there is nothing good in so doing. There is no prudence in taking part in it, and thousands of men destroy themselves in order to enjoy a moment, brief as a dream, while they gain death, so as to know it. It is a villainous intention, that of a man who thus excites himself; if he goes on to carry it out, his mind abandons him. For as for him who is without repugnance for such an act, there is no good sense at all in him.

If you desire that your conduct should be good and preserved from all evil, keep yourself from every attack of bad humor. It is a fatal malady which leads to discord, and there is no longer any existence for him who gives way to it. For it introduces discord between fathers and mothers, as well as between brothers and sisters; it causes the wife and the husband to hate each other; it contains all kinds of wickedness, it embodies all kinds of wrong. When a man has established his just equilibrium and walks in this path, there where he makes his dwelling, there is no room for bad humor.

Be not of an irritable temper as regards that which happens at your side; grumble not over your own affairs. Be not of an irritable temper in regard to your neighbors; better is a compliment to that which displeases than rudeness. It is wrong to get into a passion with one's neighbors, to be no longer master of one's words. When there is only a little irritation, one creates for oneself an affliction for the time when one will again be cool.

If you are wise, look after your house; love your wife without alloy. Fill her stomach, clothe her back; these are the cares to be bestowed on her person. Caress her, fulfil her desires during the time of her existence; it is a kindness which does honor to its possessor. Be not brutal; tact will influence her better than violence; her . . . behold to what she aspires, at what she aims, what she regards. It is that which fixes her in your house; if you repel her, it is an abyss. Open your arms for her, respond to her arms; call her, display to her your love.

Treat your dependents well, in so far as it belongs to you to do so; and it belongs to those whom Ptah has favored. If any one fails in treating his dependents well it is said: "He is a person . . ." As we do not know the events which may happen tomorrow, he is a wise person by whom one is well treated. When there comes the necessity of showing zeal, it will then be the dependents themselves who say: "Come on, come on," if good treatment has not quitted the place; if it has quitted it, the dependents are defaulters.

Do not repeat any extravagance of language; do not listen to it; it is a thing which has escaped from a hasty mouth. If it is repeated, look, without hearing it, toward the earth; say nothing in regard to it. Cause him who speaks to you to know what is just, even him who provokes to injustice; cause that which is just to be done, cause it to triumph. As for that which is hateful according to the law, condemn it by unveiling it.

If you are a wise man, sitting in the council of your lord, direct your thought toward that which is wise. Be silent rather than scatter your words. When you speak, know that which can be brought against you. To speak in the council is an art, and speech is criticized more than any other labor; it is contradiction which puts it to the proof.

If you are powerful, respect knowledge and calmness of language. Command only to direct; to be absolute is to run into evil. Let not your heart be haughty, neither let it be mean. Do not let your orders remain unsaid and cause your answers to penetrate; but speak without heat, assume a serious countenance. As for the vivacity of an ardent heart, temper it; the gentle man penetrates all obstacles. He who agitates himself all the day long has not a good moment; and he who amuses himself all the day long keeps not his fortune. Aim at fulness like pilots; once one is seated another works, and seeks to obey one's orders.

Disturb not a great man; weaken not the attention of him who is occupied. His care is to embrace his task, and he strips his person through the love which he puts into it. That transports men to Ptah, even the love for the work which they accomplish. Compose then your face even in trouble, that peace may be with you, when agitation is with . . . These are the people who succeed in what they desire.

Teach others to render homage to a great man. If you gather the crop for him among men, cause it to return fully to its owner, at whose hands is your subsistence. But the gift of affection is worth more than the provisions with which your back is covered. For that which the great man receives from you will enable your house to live, without speaking of the maintenance you enjoy, which you desire to preserve; it is thereby that he extends a beneficent hand, and that in your home good things are added to good things. Let your love pass into the heart of those who love you; cause those about you to be loving and obedient.

If you are a son of the guardians deputed to watch over the public tranquillity, execute your commission without knowing its meaning, and speak with firmness. Substitute not for that which the instructor has said what you believe to be his intention; the great use words as it suits them. Your part is to transmit rather than to comment upon.

If you are annoyed at a thing, if you are tormented by someone who is acting within his right, get out of his sight, and remember him no more when he has ceased to address you.

If you have become great after having been little, if you have become rich after having been poor, when you are at the head of the city, know how not to take advantage of the fact that you have reached the first rank, harden not your heart because of your elevation; you are become only the administrator, the prefect, of the provisions which belong to Ptah. Put not behind you the neighbor who is like you; be unto him as a companion.

Bend your back before your superior. You are attached to the palace of the king; your house is established in its fortune, and your profits are as is fitting. Yet a man is annoyed at having an authority above himself, and passes the period of life in being vexed thereat. Although that hurts not your . . . Do not plunder the house of your neighbors, seize not by force the goods which are beside you. Exclaim not then against that which you hear, and do not feel humiliated. It is necessary to reflect when one is hindered by it that the pressure of authority is felt also by one's neighbor.

Do not make . . . you know that there are obstacles to the water which comes to its hinder part, and that there is no trickling of that which is in its bosom. Let it not . . . after having corrupted his heart.

If you aim at polished manners, call not him whom you accost. Converse with him especially in such a way as not to annoy him. Enter on a discussion with him only after having left him time to saturate his mind with the subject of the conversation. If he lets his ignorance display itself, and if he gives you all opportunity to disgrace him, treat him with courtesy rather; proceed not to drive him into a corner; do not . . . the word to him; answer not in a crushing manner; crush him not; worry him not; in order that in his turn he may not return to the subject, but depart to the profit of your conversation.

Let your countenance be cheerful during the time of your existence. When we see one departing from the storehouse who has entered in order to bring his share of provision, with his face contracted, it shows that his stomach is empty and that authority is offensive to him. Let not that happen to you; it is . . .

Know those who are faithful to you when you are in low estate. Your merit then is worth more than those who did you honor. His . . ., behold that which a man possesses completely. That is of more importance than his high rank; for this is a matter which passes from one to another. The merit of one's son is advantageous to the father, and that which he really is, is worth more than the remembrance of his father's rank.

Distinguish the superintendent who directs from the workman, for manual labor is little elevated; the inaction of the hands is honorable. If a man is not in the evil way, that which places him there is the want of subordination to authority.

If you take a wife, do not . . . Let her be more contented than any of her fellow-citizens. She will be attached to you doubly, if her chain is pleasant. Do not repel her; grant that which pleases her; it is to her contentment that she appreciates your work.

If you hear those things which I have said to you, your wisdom will be fully advanced. Although they are the means which are suitable for arriving at the maat, and it is that which makes them precious, their memory would recede from the mouth of men. But thanks to the beauty of their arrangement in rhythm all their words will now be carried without alteration over this earth eternally. That will create a canvass to be embellished, whereof the great will speak, in order to instruct men in its sayings. After having listened to them the pupil will become a master, even he who shall have properly listened to the sayings because he shall have heard them. Let him win success by placing himself in the first rank; that is for him a position perfect and durable, and he has nothing further to desire forever. By knowledge his path is assured, and he is made happy by it on the earth. The wise man is satiated by knowledge; he is a great man through his own merits. His tongue is in accord with his mind; just are his lips when he speaks, his eyes when he gazes, his ears when he hears. The advantage of his son is to do that which is just without deceiving himself.

To attend therefore profits the son of him who has attended. To attend is the result of the fact that one has attended. A teachable auditor is formed, because I have attended. Good when he has attended, good when he speaks, he who has attended has profited, and it is profitable to attend to him who has attended. To attend is worth more than anything else, for it produces love, the good thing that is twice good. The son who accepts the instruction of his father will grow old on that account. What Ptah loves is that one should attend; if one attends not, it is abhorrent to Ptah. The heart makes itself its own master when it attends and when it does not attend; but if it attends, then his heart is a beneficent master to a man. In attending to instruction, a man loves what he attends to, and to do that which is prescribed is pleasant. When a son attends to his father, it is a twofold joy for both; when wise things are prescribed to him, the son is gentle toward his master. Attending to him who has attended when such things have been prescribed to him, he engraves upon his heart that which is approved by his father; and the recollection of it is preserved in the mouth of the living who exist upon this earth.

When a son receives the instruction of his father there is no error in all his plans. Train your son to be a teachable man whose wisdom is agreeable to the great. Let him direct his mouth according to that which has been said to him; in the docility of a son is discovered his wisdom. His conduct is perfect while error carries away the unteachable. Tomorrow knowledge will support him, while the ignorant will be destroyed.

As for the man without experience who listens not, he effects nothing whatsoever. He sees knowledge in ignorance, profit in loss; he commits all kinds of error, always accordingly choosing the contrary of what is praiseworthy. He lives on that which is mortal, in this fashion. His food is evil words, whereat he is filled with astonishment. That which the great know to be mortal he lives upon every day, flying from that which would be profitable to him, because of the multitude of errors which present themselves before him every day.

A son who attends is like a follower of Horus; he is happy after having attended. He becomes great, he arrives at dignity, he gives the same lesson to his children. Let none innovate upon the precepts of his father; let the same precepts form his lessons to his children. "Verily," will his children say to him, "to accomplish what you say works marvels." Cause therefore that to flourish which is just, in order to nourish your children with it. If the teachers allow themselves to be led toward evil principles, verily the people who understand them not will speak accordingly, and that being said to those who are docile they will act accordingly. Then all the world considers them as masters and they inspire confidence in the public; but their glory endures not so long as would please them. Take not away then a word from the ancient teaching, and add not one; put not one thing in place of another; beware of uncovering the rebellious ideas which arise in you; but teach according to the words of the wise. Attend if you wish to dwell in the mouth of those who shall attend to your words, when you have entered upon the office of master, that your words may be upon our lips . . . and that there may be a chair from which to deliver your arguments.

Let your thoughts be abundant, but let your mouth be under restraint, and you shall argue with the great. Put yourself in unison with the ways of your master; cause him to say: "He is my son," so that those who shall hear it shall say "Praise be to her who has borne him to him!" Apply yourself while you speak;

speak only of perfect things; and let the great who shall hear you say: "Twice good is that which issues from his mouth!"

Do that which your master bids you. Twice good is the precept of his father, from whom he has issued, from his flesh. What he tells us, let it be fixed in our heart; to satisfy him greatly let us do for him more than he has prescribed. Verily a good son is one of the gifts of Ptah, a son who does even better than he has been told to do. For his master he does what is satisfactory, putting himself with all his heart on the part of right. So I shall bring it about that your body shall be healthful, that the Pharaoh shall be satisfied with you in all circumstances and that you shall obtain years of life without default. It has caused me on earth to obtain one hundred and ten years of life, along with the gift of the favor of the Pharoah among the first of those whom their works have ennobled, satisfying the Pharoah in a place of dignity.

It is finished, from its beginning to its end, according to that which is found in writing.[1]

---

[1] From: Charles F. Horne, The Sacred Books and Early Literature of the East (New York: Parke, Austin, & Lipscomb, 1917), Vol. II: Egypt, pp. 62-78

The Instruction of Amenemope

Introduction

The beginning of the instruction about life,
   The guide for well-being,
All the principles of official procedure,
   The duties of the courtiers;
To know how to refute the accusation of one who made it,
   And to send back a reply to the one who wrote,
To set one straight on the paths of life,
   And make him prosper on earth;
To let his heart settle down in its chapel,
   As one who steers him clear of evil;
To save him from the talk of others,
   As one who is respected in the speech of men.

Written by the superintendent of the land, experienced in his office,
   The offspring of a scribe of the Beloved Land,
The Superintendent of produce, who fixes the grain measure,
   Who sets the grain tax amount for his lord,
Who registers the islands which appear as new land over the cartouche of His Majesty,
   And sets up the land mark at the boundary of the arable land,
Who protects the king by his tax rolls,
   And makes the Register of the Black land.
The scribe who places the divine offerings for all the gods,
   The donor of land grants to the people,
The superintendent of grain who administers the food offerings,
   Who supplies the storerooms with grain
A truly silent man in Tjeni in the Ta-wer nome,
   One whose verdict is "acquitted" in Ipu,
The owner of a pyramid tomb on the west of Senut,

As well as the owner of a memorial chapel in Abydos,
Amenemope, the son of Kanakht,
    Whose verdict is "acquitted" in the Ta-wer nome.

For his son, the youngest of his children,
    The least of his family,
Initiate of the mysteries of Min-Kamutef,
    Libation pourer of Wennofre,
Who introduces Horus upon the throne of his father,
    His stolist in his august chapel,

    The seer of the Mother of God,
The inspector of the black cattle of the terrace of Min,
    Who protects Min in his chapel,
Hoermmaakheru is his true name,
    A child of an official of Ipu,
The son of the sistrum player of Shu and Tefnut,
    The chief singer of Horus, the Lady Tawosret.

He Says:

Chapter I

Give your years and hear what is said,
    Give your mind over to their interpretation:
It is profitable to put them in your heart,
    But woe to him that neglects them!
Let them rest in the shrine of your insides
    That they may act as a lock in your heart;
Now when there comes a storm of words,
    They will be a mooring post on your tongue.

If you spend a lifetime with these things in your heart,
    You will find it good fortune;
You will discover my words to be a treasure house of life,
    And your body will flourish upon earth.

Chapter 2

Beware of stealing from a miserable man
    And of raging against the cripple.
Do not stretch out your hand to touch an old man,
    Nor snip at the words of an elder.
Don't let yourself be involved in a fraudulent business,
    Not desire the carrying out of it;
Do not get tired because of being interfered with,
    Nor return an answer on your own.
The evildoer, throw him in the canal,
    And he will bring back its slime.
The north wind comes down and ends his appointed hour,
    It is joined to the tempest;
The thunder is high, the crocodiles are nasty,
    O hot-headed man, what are you like?
he cries out, and his voice reaches heaven.
    O Moon, make his crime manifest!
Row that we may ferry the evil man away,
    For we will not act according to his evil nature;
Lift him up, give him your hand,
    And leave him in the hands of god;
Fill his gut with your own food
    That he may be sated and ashamed.
Something else of value in the heart of God
    Is to stop and think before speaking.

Chapter 3

Do not get into a quarrel with the argumentative man
    Nor incite him with words;
Proceed cautiously before an opponent,
    And give way to an adversary;
Sleep on it before speaking,
    For a storm come forth like fire in hay is

The hot-headed man in his appointed time.
    May you be restrained before him;
Leave him to himself,
    And God will know how to answer him.

If you spend your life with these things in your heart,
    Your children shall behold them.

Chapter 4

The hot-headed man in the temple
    Is like a tree grown indoors;
Only for a moment does it put forth roots.
    It reaches its end in the carpentry shop,
It is floated away far from its place,
    Or fire is its funeral pyre.

the truly temperate man sets himself apart,
    He is like a tree grown in a sunlit field,
But it flourishes, it doubles its yield,
    It stands before its owner;
Its fruit is something sweet, its shade is pleasant,
    And it reaches its end as a statue.

Chapter 5

Do not take by violence the shares of the temple,
    Do not be grasping, and you will find overabundance;
Do not take away a temple servant
    In order to acquire the property of another man.
Do not say today is the same as tomorrow,
    Or how will matters come to pass?
When tomorrow comes, today is past;
    The deep waters sink from the canal bank,
Crocodiles are uncovered, the hippopotamuses are on dry land,

And the fishes gasping for air;
The wolves are fat, the wild fowl in festival,
And the nets are drained.

Every temperate man in the temple says,
"Great is the benevolence of Re."
Fill yourself with silence, you will find life,
And your body shall flourish upon earth.

Chapter 6

Do not displace the surveyor's marker on the boundaries of the arable land,
Nor alter the position of the measuring line;
Do not be greedy for a plot of land,
Nor overturn the boundaries of a widow.

As for the road in the field worn down by time,
He who takes it violently for fields,
If he traps by deceptive attestations,
Will be lassoed by the might of the moon.

To one who has done this on earth, pay attention,
For he is a weak enemy;
He is an enemy overturned inside himself;
Life is taken from his eye;
His household is hostile to the community,
His storerooms are toppled over,
His property taken from his children,
And to someone else his possessions given.

Take care not to topple over the boundary marks of the arable land,
Not fearing that you will be brought to court;
Man propitiates God by the might of the Lord
When he sets straight the boundaries of the arable land.

Desire, then, to make yourself prosper,
    And take care for the Lord of All;
Do not trample on the furrow of someone else,
    Their good order will be profitable for you.

So plough the fields, and you will find whatever you need,
    And receive the bread from your own threshing floor:
Better is the bushel which God gives you
    Than five thousand deceitfully gotten;
They do not spend a day in the storehouse or warehouse,
    They are no use for dough for beer;
Their stay in the granary is short-lived,
    When morning comes they will be swept away.
Better, then, is poverty in the hand of God
    Than riches in the storehouse;
Better is bread when the mind is at ease
    Than riches with anxiety.

Chapter 7

Do not set your heart upon seeking riches,
    For there is no one who can ignore Destiny and Fortune;
Do not set your thoughts on external matters:
    For every man there is his appointed time.

Do not exert yourself to seek out excess
    And your wealth will prosper for you;
If riches come to you by theft
    They will not spend the night with you;
As soon as day breaks they will not be in your household;
    Although their places can be seen, they are not there.

When the earth opens up its mouth, it levels him and swallows him up,
    And it drowns him in the deep;

They have made for themselves a great hole which suites them.
> And they have sunk themselves in the tomb;

Or they have made themselves wings like geese,
> And they fly up to the sky.

Do not be pleased with yourself because of riches acquired through robbery,
> Neither complain about poverty.

If an officer commands one who goes in front of him,
> His company leaves him;

The boat of the covetous is abandoned in the mud,
> While the skiff of the truly temperate man sails on.

When he rises you shall offer to the Aten,
> Saying, "Grant me prosperity and health."

And he will give you your necessities for life,
> And you will be safe from fear.

Chapter 8

Set your good deeds throughout the world
> That you may greet everyone;

They make rejoicing for the Uraeus,
> And spit against the Apophis.

Keep your tongue safe from words of detraction,
> And you will be the loved one of the people,

Then you will find your place within the temple
> And your offerings among the bread deliveries of your lord;

You will be revered, when you are concealed in your grave,
> And be safe from the might of God.

Do not accuse a man,
> When the news of an escape is concealed.

If you hear something good or bad,
> Say it outside, where it is not heard;

Set a good report on your tongue,

While the bad thing is covered up inside you.

Chapter 9

Do not fraternize with the hot-tempered man,
    Nor approach him to converse.
Safeguard your tongue from answering your superior,
    And take care not to speak against him.
Do not allow him to cast words only to entrap you,
    And be not too free in your reply;
With a man of your own station discuss the reply;
    And take care of speaking thoughtlessly;
When a man's heart is upset, words travel faster
    Than wind and rain.

He is ruined and created by his tongue,
    And yet he speaks slander;
He makes an answer deserving of a beating,
    For its work is evil;
He sails among all the world,
    But his cargo is false words;
He acts the ferryman in knitting words:
    He goes forth and comes back arguing.

But whether he eats or whether he drinks inside,
    His accusation waits for him without.
They day when his evil deed is brought to court
    Is a disaster for his children.
Even Khnum will straightway come, even Khnum will straightway come,
    The creator of the ill-tempered man
Whom he molds and fires....;
    He is like a wolf cub in the farmyard,
And he turns one eye to the other squinting,
    For he sets families to argue.
He goes before all the wind like clouds,

He darkens his color in the sun;
He crocks his tail like a baby crocodile,
    He curls himself up to inflict harm,
His lips are sweet, but his tongue is bitter,
    And fire burns inside him.

Do not fly up to join that man
    Not fearing you will be brought to account.

Chapter 10

Do not address your intemperate friend in your unrighteousness,
    Nor destroy your own mind;
Do not say to him, "May you be praised,: not meaning it
    When there is fear within you.
Do not converse falsely with a man,
    For it is the abomination of God.
Do not separate your mind from your tongue,
    All your plans will succeed.
You will be important before others,
    While you will be secure in the hand of God.

God hates one who falsified words,
    His great abomination is duplicity.

Chapter 11

Do not covet the property of the dependent
    Nor hunger for his bread;
The property of a dependent blocks the throat,
    It is vomit for the gullet.
If he has engendered it by false oaths,
    His heart slips back inside him.
It is through the disaffected that success is lost,
    Bad and good elude.

If you are at a loss before your superior,
    And are confused in your speeches,
Your flattering are turned back with curses,
    And your humble action by beatings.
Whoever fills the mouth with too much bread swallows it and spits up,
    So he is emptied of his good.

To the examination of a dependant give thought
    While the sticks touch him,
And while all his people are fettered with manacles:
    Who is to have the execution?
When you are too free before your superior,
    Then you are in bad favor with your subordinates,
So steer away from the poor man on the road,
    That you may see him but keep clear of his property.

Chapter 12

Do not covet the property of an official,
    And do not fill your mouth with too much food extravagantly;
    If he sets you to manage his property,
    Respect his, and yours will prosper.

Do not deal with the intemperate man,
    Nor associate yourself to a disloyal party.

If you are sent to transport straw,
    Respect its account;
If a man is detected in a dishonest transaction,
    Never again will he be employed.

Chapter 13

Do not lead a man astray with reed pen or papyrus document:
    It is the abomination of God.
Do not witness a false statement,
    Nor remove a man from the list by your order;
Do not enroll someone who has nothing,
    Nor make your pen be false.
If you find a large debt against a poor man,
    Make it into three parts;
Release two of them and let one remain:
    You will find it a path of life;
You will pass the night in sound sleep; in the morning
    You will find it like good news.

Better it is to be praised as one loved by men
    Than wealth in the storehouse;
Better is bread when the mind is at ease
    Than riches with troubles.

Chapter 14

Do not pay attention to a person,
    Nor exert yourself to seek out his hand,
If he says to you, "take a bribe,"
    It is not an insignificant matter to heed him;
Do not avert your glance from him, nor bend down your head,
    Nor turn aside your gaze.
Address him with your words and say to him greetings;
    When he stops, your chance will come;
Do not repel him at his first approach,
    Another time he will be brought to judgment.

Chapter 15

Do well, and you will attain influence.
    Do not dip your reed against the one who sins.
The beak of the Ibis is the finger of the scribe;
    Take care not to disturb it;
The Ape Thoth rests in the temple of Khmun,
    While his eye travels around the Two Lands;
If he sees one who sins with his finger that is, a false scribe,
    he takes away his provisions by the flood.
As for a scribe who sins with his finger,
His son shall not be enrolled.

If you spend your life with these things in your heart,
    Your children shall see them.

Chapter 16

Do not unbalance the scale nor make the weights false,
    Nor diminish the fractions of the grain measure;
Do not wish for the grain measures of the fields
    And then cast aside those of the treasury.
The Ape sits by the balance,
    While his heart is the plummet.
Where is a god as great as Thoth
    The one who discovered these things, to create them?

Do not get for yourself short weights;
    They are plentiful, yea, an army by the might of God.
If you see someone cheating,
    At a distance you must pass him by.
Do not be avaricious for copper,
    And abjure fine clothes;
What good is one cloaked in fine linen woven as mek,
    When he cheats before God.
When gold is heaped upon gold,

At daybreak it turns to lead.

Chapter 17

Beware of robbing the grain measure
    To falsify its fractions;
Do not act wrongfully through force,
    Although it is empty inside;
May you have it measure exactly as to its size,
    Your hand stretching out with precision.

Make not for yourself a measure of two capacities,
    For then it is toward the depths that you will go.
The measure is the eye of Re,
    Its abomination is the one who takes.
As for a grain measurer who multiplies and subtracts,
    His eye will seal up against him.

Do not receive the harvest tax of a cultivator,
    Nor bind up a papyrus against him to lead him astray.
Do not enter into collusion with the grain measurer,
    Nor play with the seed allotment,
More important is the threshing floor for barley
    Than swearing by the Great Throne.

Chapter 18

Do not go to bed fearing tomorrow,
    For when day breaks what is tomorrow?
Man knows not what tomorrow is!
God is success,
    Man is failure.
The words which men say pass on one side,
    The things which God does pass on another side.

Do not say, "I am without fault,"

Nor try to seek out trouble.
Fault is the business of God,
    It is locked up with his seal.
There is no success in the hand of God,
    Nor is there failure before Him;
If he turns himself about to seek out success,
    In a moment He destroys him.

Be strong in your heart, make your mind firm,
    Do not steer with your tongue;
The tongue of a man is the steering oar of a boat,
    And the Lord of All is its pilot.

Chapter 19

Do not enter the council chamber in the presence of a magistrate
    And then falsify your speech.
Do not go up and down with your accusation
    When your witnesses stand readied.
Do not overstate through oaths in the name of your lord,
    Through pleas in the place of questioning.

Tell the truth before the magistrate,
    lest he gain power over your body;
If you come before him the next day,
    He will concur with all you say;
He will present your case in court before the Council of the Thirty,
    And it will be lenient another time as well.

Chapter 20

Do not corrupt the people of the law court,
    Nor put aside the just man,
Do not agree because of garments of white,

    Nor accept one in rags.
Take not the gift of the strong man,
    Nor repress the weak for him.
Justice is a wonderful gift of God,
    And He will render it to whomever he wishes.
The strength of one like him
    Saves a poor wretch from his beatings.

Do not make false enrollment lists,
    For they are a serious affair deserving death;
They are serious oaths of the kind promising not to misuse an office,
    And they are to be investigated by an informer.

Do not falsify the oracles on a papyrus
    And thereby alter the designs of God.
Do not arrogate to yourself the might of God
    As if Destiny and Fortune did not exist.

Hand property over to its rightful owners,
    And seek out life for yourself;
Let not your heart build in their house,
    for then your neck will be on the execution block.

Chapter 21

Do not say, I have found a strong protector
    And now I can challenge a man in my town.
Do not say, I have found an active intercessor,
    And now I can challenge him whom I hate.

Indeed, you cannot know the plans of God;
    You cannot perceive tomorrow.
Sit yourself at the hands of God:
    Your tranquility will cause them to open.

As for the crocodile deprived of his tongue,
    the fear of him is negligible.
Empty not your soul to everybody
    And do not diminish thereby your importance;
Do not circulate your words to others,
    Nor fraternize with one who is too candid.

Better is a man whose knowledge is inside him
    Than one who talks to disadvantage.
One cannot run to attain perfection;
    One cannot create only to destroy it.

Chapter 22

Do not castigate your companion in a dispute,
    And do not let him say his innermost thoughts;
Do not fly up to greet him
    When you do not see how he acts.
May you first comprehend his accusation
    And cool down your opponent.

Leave it to him and he will empty his soul;
    Sleep knows how to find him out;
Take his feet, do not bother him;
    Fear him, do not underestimate him.
Indeed, you cannot know the plans of God,
    You cannot perceive tomorrow.
Sit yourself at the hands of God;
    Your tranquility will cause them to open.

Chapter 23

Do not eat a meal in the presence of a magistrate,
    Nor set to speaking first.
If you are satisfied with false words,
    Enjoy yourself with your spittle.

Look at the cup in front of you,
    And let it suffice your need.
Even as a noble is important in his office,
    He is like the abundance of a well when it is drawn.

Chapter 24

Do not listen to the accusation of an official indoors,
    And then repeat it to another outside.
Do not allow your discussions to be brought outside
    So that your heart will not be grieved.

the heart of a man is the beak of the God,
    So take care not to slight it;
A man who stands at the side of an official
    Should not have his name known in the street.

Chapter 25

Do not jeer at a blind man nor tease a dwarf,
    Neither interfere with the condition of a cripple;
Do not taunt a man who is in the hand of God,
    Nor scowl at him if he errs.

Man is clay and straw,
    And God is his potter;
He overthrows and he builds daily,
    He impoverishes a thousand if He wishes.
He makes a thousand into examiners,
    When He is in His hour of life.
How fortunate is he who reaches the West,
    When he is safe in the hand of God.

Chapter 26

Do not stay in the tavern
    And join someone greater than you,
Whether he be high or low in his station,
    An old man or a youth;
But take as a friend for yourself someone compatible:
    Re is helpful though he is far away.

When you see someone greater than you outside,
    And attendants following him, respect him.
And give a hand to an old man filled with beer:
    Respect him as his children would.

The strong arm is not weakened when it is uncovered,
    The back is not broken when one bends it;
Better is the poor man who speaks sweet words,
    Than the rich man who speaks harshly.

A pilot who sees into the distance
    Will not let his ship capsize.

Chapter 27

Do not reproach someone older than you,
    For he has seen the Sun before you;
Do not let yourself be reported to the Aten when he rises,
    With the words, "Another young man has reproached an elder."
    Very sick in the sight of Re
        Is a young man who reproaches an elder.

Let him beat you with your hands folded,
    Let him reproach you while you keep quiet.
Then when you come before him in the morning
    He will give you bread freely.

As for bread, he who has it becomes a dog,
    He barks to the one who gives it.

Chapter 28

Do not expose a widow if you have caught her in the fields,
    Nor fail to give way if she is accused.
Do not turn a stranger away from your oil jar
    That it may be made double for your family.
God loves him who cares for the poor,
    More than him who respects the wealthy.

Chapter 29

Do not turn people away from crossing the river
    When you have room in your ferryboat;
If a steering oar is given you in the midst of the deep waters,
    So bend back your hands to take it up.
It is not an abomination in the hand of God
    If the passenger is not cared for.

Do not acquire a ferryboat on the river,
    And then attempt to seek out its fares;
Take the are from the man of means,
    But also accept the destitute without charge.

Chapter 30

Mark for your self these thirty chapters:
    They please, they instruct,
They are the foremost of all books;
    They teach the ignorant.
If they are read to an ignorant man,
    He will be purified through them.
Seize them; put them in your mind
    And have men interpret them, explaining as a teacher.

As to a scribe who is experienced in his position,
   He will find himself worthy of being a courtier.

[Colophon]

It is finished.
By the writing of Senu, son of the god's father Pamiu.

The Loyalist Instruction from the Sehetepibre Stela

I have something important to say; I shall have you hear it, and I shall let you know it: the design for eternity, a way of life as it should be and of passing a lifetime at peace.
Adore the king, Nymaatre, living forever, in your innermost parts.
Place His Majesty in friendly fashion in your thoughts.
He is perception, which is in all hearts, and his eyes piece through every being.
He is Re, by whose rays one sees, for he is one who illumines the Two Lands more than the sun disk.
he is one who makes the land green, even more than a high inundation: he has filled the Two Lands with victory and life.
Nostrils are cool when he starts to rage, but when he sets in peace, one can breathe the air again.
He gives nourishment to those in his circle, and he feeds the one who sticks to his path.
The king is Ka.
His utterance is Abundance.
The one whom he brought up is one who will be somebody.
His is Khnum for all limbs,
| The Begetter of the begotten.
He is Bastet, who protects the Two Lands.
The one who praises him will be protected by his arm.
He is Sakhmet, against those who disobey his orders, and the one with whom he disagrees will be laden with sorrow.
Fight on behalf of his name: be obeisant to his life. Be free and clear of any instance of negligence.
The one whom the king loves shall be a well provided spirit; there is no tomb for anyone who rebels against His Majesty, and his corpse shall be cast to the waters.
Do this, and your body will flourish, and you will find it excellent for eternity.

The Instructions of Dua-Khety

The beginning of the teaching which the man of Tjel named Dua-Khety made for his son named Pepy, while he sailed southwards to the Residence to place him in the school of writings among the children of the magistrates, the most eminent men of the Residence.

So he spoke to him: Since I have seen those who have been beaten, it is to writings that you must set your mind. Observe the man who has been carried off to a work force. Behold, there is nothing that surpasses writings! They are a boat upon the water. Read then at the end of the Book of Kemyet this statement in it saying: As for a scribe in any office in the Residence, he will not suffer want in it.

When he fulfills the bidding of another, he does not come forth satisfied. I do not see an office to be compared with it, to which this maxim could relate. I shall make you love books more than your mother, and I shall place their excellence before you. It is greater than any office. There is nothing like it on earth. When he began to become sturdy but was still a child, he was greeted respectfully. When he was sent to carry out a task, before he returned he was dressed in adult garments.

I do not see a stoneworker on an important errand or a in a place to which he has been sent, but I have seen a coppersmith at his work at the door of his furnace. His fingers were like the claws of the crocodile, and he stank more than fish excrement.

Every carpenter who bears the adze is wearier than a fieldhand. His field is his wood, his hoe is the axe. There is no end to his work, and he must labor excessively in his activity. At nighttime he still must light his lamp.

The jeweler pierces stone in stringing beads in all kinds of hard stone. When he has completed the inlaying of the eye-amulets, his strength vanishes and he is tired out. He sits until the arrival of the sun, his knees and his back bent at the place called Aku-Re.

The barber shaves until the end of the evening. But he must be up early, crying out, his bowl upon his arm. He takes himself from street to street to seek out someone to shave. He wears out his arms to fill his belly, like bees who eat only according to their work.

The reed-cutter goes downstream to the Delta to fetch himself arrows. He must work excessively in his activity. When the gnats sting him and the sand fleas bite him as well, then he is judged.

The potter is covered with earth, although his lifetime is still among the living. He burrows in the field more than swine to bake his cooking vessels. His clothes being stiff with mud, his head cloth consists only of rags, so that the air which comes forth from his burning furnace enters his nose. He operates a pestle with his feet with which he himself is pounded, penetrating the courtyard of every house and driving earth into every open place.

I shall also describe to you the bricklayer. His kidneys are painful. When he must be outside in the wind, he lays bricks without a garment. His belt is a cord for his back, a string for his buttocks. His strength has vanished through fatigue and stiffness, kneading all his excrement. He eats bread with his fingers, although he washes himself but once a day.

It is miserable for the carpenter when he planes the roof-beam. It is the roof of a chamber 10 by 6 cubits. A month goes by in laying the beams and spreading the matting. All the work is accomplished. But as for the food which is to be given to his household while he is away, there is no one who provides for his children.

The vintner carries his shoulder-yoke. Each of his shoulders is burdened with age. A swelling is on his neck, and it festers. He spends the morning in watering leeks and the evening with corianders, after he has spent the midday in the palm grove. So it happens that he sinks down at last and dies through his deliveries, more than one of any other profession.

The fieldhand cries out more than the guinea fowl. His voice is louder than the raven's. His fingers have become ulcerous with an excess of stench. When he is taken away to be enrolled in Delta labour, he is in tatters. He suffers when he proceeds to the island, and sickness is his payment. The forced labour then is tripled. If he comes back from the marshes there, he reaches his house worn out, for the forced labor has ruined him.

The weaver inside the weaving house is more wretched than a woman. His knees are drawn up against his belly. He cannot breathe the air. If he wastes a single day without weaving, he is beaten with 50 whip lashes. He has to give food to the doorkeeper to allow him to come out to the daylight.

The arrow maker, completely wretched, goes into the desert. Greater than his own pay is what he has to spend for his she-ass for its work afterwards. Great is also what he has to give to the fieldhand to set him on the right road to the flint source. When he reaches his house in the evening, the journey has ruined him.

The courier goes abroad after handing over his property to his children, being fearful of the lions and the Asiatics. He only knows himself when he is back in Egypt. But his household by then is only a tent. There is no happy homecoming.

The furnace-tender, his fingers are foul, the smell thereof is as corpses. His eyes are inflamed because of the heaviness of smoke. He cannot get rid of his dirt, although he spends the day at the reed pond. Clothes are an abomination to him.

The sandal maker is utterly wretched carrying his tubs of oil. His stores are provided with carcasses, and what he bites is hides.

The washerman launders at the riverbank in the vicinity of the crocodile. I shall go away, father, from the flowing water, said his son and his daughter, to a more satisfactory profession, one more distinguished than any other profession. His food is mixed with filth, and there is no part of him which is clean. He cleans the clothes of a woman in menstruation. He weeps when he spends all day with a beating stick and a stone there. One says to him, dirty laundry, come to me, the brim overflows.

The fowler is utterly weak while searching out for the denizens of the sky. If the flock passes by above him, then he says:

would that I might have nets. But God will not let this come to pass for him, for He is opposed to his activity.

I mention for you also the fisherman. He is more miserable than one of any other profession, one who is at his work in a river infested with crocodiles. When the totalling of his account is made for him, then he will lament. One did not tell him that a crocodile was standing there, and fear has now blinded him. When he comes to the flowing water, so he falls as through the might of God.

See, there is no office free from supervisors, except the scribe's. He is the supervisor!

But if you understand writings, then it will be better for you than the professions which I have set before you. Behold the official and the dependent pertaining to him. The tenant farmer of a man cannot say to him: Do not keep watching me. What I have done in journeying southward to the Residence is what I have done through love of you. A day at school is advantageous to you. Seek out its work early, while the workmen I have caused you to know hurry on and cause the recalcitrant to hasten.

I will also tell you another matter to teach you what you should know at the station of your debating. Do not come close to where there is a dispute. If a man reproves you, and you do not know how to oppose his anger, make your reply cautiously in the presence of listeners.

If you walk to the rear of officials, approach from a distance behind the last. If you enter while the master of the house is at home, and his hands are extended to another in front of you, sit with your hand to your mouth. Do not ask for anything in his presence. But do as he says to you. Beware of approaching the table.

Be serious, and great as to your worth. Do not speak secret matters. For he who hides his innermost thoughts is one who makes a shield for himself. Do not utter thoughtless words when you sit down with an angry man.

When you come forth from school after midday recess has been announced to you, go into the courtyard and discuss the last part of your lesson book.

When an official sends you as a messenger, then say what he said. Neither take away nor add to it. He who abandons a chest of books, his name will not endure. He who is wise in all his ways, nothing will be hidden from him, and he will not be rebuffed from any station of his.

Do not say anything false about your mother. This is an abomination to the officials. The offspring who does useful things, his condition is equal to the one of yesterday. Do not indulge with an undisciplined man, for it is bad after it is heard about you. When you have eaten three loaves of bread and swallowed two jugs of beer, and the body has not yet had enough, fight against it. But if another is satiated, do not stand, take care not to approach the table.

See, you send out a large number. You hear the words of the officials. Then you may assume the characteristics of the children of men, and you may walk in their footsteps. One values a scribe for his understanding, for understanding transforms an eager person. You are to stand when words of welcome are offered. Your feet shall not hurry when you walk. Do not approach a trusted man, but associate with one more distinguished than you. But let you friend be a man of your generation.

See, I have placed you on the path of God. The fate of a man is on his shoulders on the day he is born. He comes to the judgement hall and the court of magistrates which the people have made. See, there is no scribe lacking sustenance, or the provisions of the royal house. It is Meskhenet who is turned toward the scribe who presents himself before the court of magistrates. Honour your father and mother who have placed you on the path of the living. Mark this, which I have placed before your eyes, and the children of your children.

It has come to an end in peace.

The Teaching for Merikare

[here begins the teaching which King...made] for his son Merikare [...]. As for [...] his kinsfolk [...] the citizens [...] him, and his partisans are many in sum [...] enter [...] he is pleasing in the sight of his serfs, being firmly established in [...]. A talker is a mischief-maker, suppress him, kill [him], erase his name, [destroy] his kinsfolk, suppress the remembrance of him and his partisans who love him.

A violent man is a confuser of the citizens who always makes partisans of the younger generation. If now you find someone belonging to the citizenry [...] and his deeds have passed beyond you, accuse him before the entourage and suppress [him], for he is a rebel indeed; a talker is a mischief-maker. Bend the multitude and drive out hot temper from it; [...] will not rise [in] rebellion by means of the poor man when he is made to rebel.

[The mind] of the underling is confused; the army [...]; put an end to it by mixing [...]. Many are angry, for men are put in the labor establishment. Be lenient [...] when you oppose; when you fatten [herds, the people] are in joy. Justify yourself in the presence of God; then men will say [...] you [plan]. You shall contend against wrong [...] a good disposition is a man's heaven, but vilification by the ill-disposed man is dangerous.

Be skillful in speech, that you may be strong; [...] it is the strength of [...] the tongue, and words are braver than all fighting; none can circumvent the clever man [...] on the mat; a wise man is a [school] for the magnates, and those who are aware of his knowledge do not attack him. [Falsehood] does not exist near him, but truth comes to him in full essence, after the manner of what the ancestors said.

Copy your forefathers, for [work] is carried out through knowledge; see, their words endure in writing. Open, that you may read and copy knowledge; even the expert will become one who is instructed. Do not be evil, for patience is good; make your lasting monument in the love of you. Multiply [the people] whom the city has enfolded; then will God be praised because of rewards; men will watch over your [...] and give thanks for your goodness, and your health will be prayed for [...].

Respect the great; keep your people safe; consolidate your frontier and your patrolled area, for it is good to work for the future. Show respect [...] life for the clear-sighted, but the trusting man will suffer pain. Let men be sent [...] through your kindly disposition. Wretched is he who has bound the land to himself [...] a fool is he who is greedy when others posses. [Life] on earth passes away, it is not long; he is fortunate who [has a good] remembrance in it. No man goes straight forward, even though a million belong to the Lord of the Two Lands. [...] shall live forever; he who comes from the hand of Osiris shall depart, just as he who is self-indulgent shall be lost.

Make your magnates great, that they may execute your laws; one who is rich in his house will not be one-sided, for he who does not lack is an owner of property; a poor man does not speak truly, and one who says, "Would that I had,' is not straightforward; he is one-sided toward the possessor of rewards. Great is the great one whose great ones are great; valiant is a king who owns an entourage; and august is he who is rich in magnates. Speak truth in your house, so that the magnates who are on earth may respect you, for a sovereign's renown lies in straightforwardness; it is the front room of a house that inspires the back room with respect.

Do justice, that you may live long upon earth. Calm the weeper, do not oppress the widow, do not oust a man from his father's property, do not degrade magnates from their seats. Beware of punishing wrongfully; do not kill, for it will not profit you, but punish with beatings and with imprisonment, for thus the land will be set in order, excepting only the rebel who has conspired, for God knows those who are disaffected, and God will smite down his evil doing with blood. It is the lenient man who [...] lifetime; so do not kill a man of whose ability you are aware, and with whom you once recited writings, but read in the account [...] because of God, and stride forward freely in a difficult place. The soul comes to the place which it knows, and it will not overstep the ways of the past; no magic can oppose it, and it will reach those who will give it water.

As for the tribunal which judges the needy, you know that they will not be lenient on that day of judging the poor; in the hour of exercising their function, wretched is he who is accused as a wise man. Do not put your trust in length of years, for they regard a lifetime as an hour; a man survives after death, and his deeds are laid before him in a heap. Existence yonder is eternal, and he who complains of it is a fool, but as for him who attains it, he will be like a god yonder, striding forward like the lords of eternity.

Raise up your young troops, that the Residence may love you. Multiply your partisans as neighbors; see, your towns are full of newly settled folk. It is for twenty years that the rising generation is happy in following its desire, and neighbors come forth again; he who is caused to enter goes in for himself by means of children [...]. Ancient times have fought for us, and I raised troops from them at my accession. Make your magnates great, promote your [warriors], increase the rising generation of your retainers, they being equipped with knowledge, established with lands, and endowed with cattle.

Do not distinguish the son of a man of rank from a commoner, but take a man to yourself because of his actions, so that every craft may be carried on [...] for the possessor of strength. Guard your frontier, marshal your fortresses, for troops are profitable to their master. Construct [fine] monuments to God, for it means the perpetuation of the name of whoever does it, and a man should do what is profitable to his soul, namely monthly service as priest and the wearing of white sandals. Enrich the fane, be discreet concerning the mysteries, enter into the sanctuary, eat bread in the temple, richly provide the altars, increase the revenues, add to the daily offerings, for it is a profitable matter for whoever does it; maintain your monuments in proportion to your wealth, for a single day gives to eternity, an hour does good for the future, and God is aware of him who serves him. Dispatch your statues to a distant land of which they shall not render an inventory, for he who destroys the goods of an enemy will suffer.

The enemy cannot be quiet even within Egypt, but troops shall subdue troops, in accordance with the prophecy of the ancestors about it, and men fight against Egypt even in the necropolis. Do not destroy ancient buildings with a destruction through action; I acted thus and so it happened, just as he who had transgressed likewise did against God. Do not deal ill with the Southern Region, for you know the prophecy of the Residence about it, and it has happened [even as] this shall happen; they shall not transgress as they said [...]. I turned back to Thinis [...] its southern boundary at Tawer, and I captured it like a cloudburst, though King Mer-[...]re did not do it. Be lenient about it....[...] renew contracts. There is no pure reason who is caused to be hidden, and it is good to act on behalf of posterity.

You stand well with the Southern Region, for the bearers of loads come to you with produce; I did the same as the ancestors, and there was none who had corn who gave it. Be kindly to those who are weak toward you, and satisfy yourself with your own bread and beer. Granite comes to you without hindrance, so do not destroy someone else's monuments. Hew stone in Turah, but do not build your tomb of what has been thrown down, or of what has been made for what is to be made. See, the king is a possessor of joy; you can be drowsy and you can sleep through your strength of arm; follow your desire through what I have done, for there is no enemy within your frontier.

I rose as ruler in my city, but I was anxious about the Delta from he-shenu to Sebak, its southern boundary being at the Canal of the Two Fishes. I pacified the west as far as the sand dunes of the Fayyum; it labors and yields meru-wood; men see wan-wood once again and yield it to us. But the east is rich in foreigners, and their taxes are [withheld]; the Middle Island is turned about, and also everyone in it. yet the temples say of me: O Great One, men salute you.

See, [the land] which they destroyed is made into districts and every great city [is restored]. The governance of each one is in the hands of ten men, a magistrate is appointed who will levy [...] the amount of all taxes. The priest is provided with a farm, and men work for you like a single gang. How is it that disaffection does not occur? Because you will not suffer from a Nile which fails to come, and the revenues of the Delta are in your hand. See, the mooring post which I have made in the east is driven in from the limits of Hebnu to Road-of-Horus, settled with towns and full of people of the pick of the entire land, to repel enemies from them. May I see a brave man who will imitate it and who will do more than I have done [...] by the hand of a cowardly heir.

Speak thus concerning the barbarian: As for the wretched Asiatic, unpleasant is the place where he is with trouble from water, difficulty from many trees, and the roads thereof awkward by reason of mountains. He does not dwell in one place, being driven hither and yon through want, going about [the desert] on foot. He has been fighting since the time of Horus; he never conquers, yet he is not conquered, and he does not announce a day of fighting, like a thief whom a community has driven out.

But I lived, and while I existed the barbarians were as though in the walls of a fortress; [my troops] broke open [...]. I caused the Delta to smite them, I carried off their people, I took away their cattle, until the detestation of the Asiatics was against Egypt. Do not worry about him, for the Asiatic is a crocodile on his riverbank; he snatches a lonely serf, but he will never rob in the vicinity of a populous town.

Dig a moat against [...] and flood the half of it at the Bitter Lakes, for see, it is the navel-string of the desert dwellers; its walls and its soldiers are many and the partisans in it know how to take up arms, apart from the freemen of the camp; the region of Djed-esut totals ten thousand men consisting of free untaxed commoners, and magnates have been in it since the time of the Residence. its boundary is established, its garrison is brave, and many northerners irrigate it to the limits of the Delta, they being taxed in corn like freemen; it is... the face of him who made it, and see, it is the door of the Delta. They made a moat for Ninsu, for a populous city is... Beware of being surrounded by the partisans of an enemy; watchfulness is what renews years.

When your frontier to the Southern Region is troubled, it is the barbarians who have taken the belt. Build castles in the Delta, for a man's name will not be diminished by what he has done, and a well-founded city cannot be harmed. Build castles [...], for an enemy loves disturbance, and his actions are mean.

The late King Akhtoy ordained in a teaching: "Be inactive about the violent man who destroys altars, for God will attack him who rebels against the temples. men will come about it according as he does it; he will be satisfied with what is ordained for him, namely a trap for him; no one will use loyalty toward him on that day of coming. protect the altars, worship God, and do not say: It is weakness of mind"; do not let your arms be loose. As for him who makes rebellion against you, it is to destroy the sky. Prosperity means a year of monuments; even if an enemy knows, he will not destroy them, through the desire that what he ahs done may be embellished by another who comes after. There is not one devoid of an enemy, but the ruler of the Two Banks is a wise man, and a king who possesses an entourage cannot act stupidly. He is wise from birth, and God will distinguish him above millions of men.

The kingship is a goodly office; it has no son and it has no brother who shall make its monuments endure, yet it is the one person who ennobles the other; a man works for his predecessor, through the desire that what he has done may be embellished by another who shall come after him. A mean act was committed in my reign; the territory of Thinis was devastated. It indeed happened, but not through what I had done; I knew of it only after it was done. See, the consequences exceeded what I had done, for what is damaged is spoiled, and there is no benefit for him who restores what he himself has ruined, who demolishes what he ahs built and embellished what he has defaced; beware of it! A blow is repaid by the like of it, and all that is achieved is a hitting.

One generation of men passes to another, and God, who knows character, has hidden Himself. There is none who will oppose the possessor of a hand, and he is an attacker of what the eyes see, so worship God upon his way. Things are made of costly stone and fashioned in copper; the mud flat is replaced with water; there is no stream that can be made to hide, for it means that the dike in which it hid itself is destroyed. The soul goes to the place it knows and does not stray on yesterday's road. Beautify your mansion in the West, embellish your place in the necropolis with straightforwardness and just dealing, for it is on that which their hearts rely; more acceptable is the character of the straightforward man than the ox of the wrongdoer. Serve God, that he may do the like for you, with offerings for replenishing the altars and with carving; it is that which will show forth your name, and God is aware of whoever serves Him. Provide for men, the cattle of God, for he made heaven and earth at their desire. He suppressed the greed of the waters, he gave the breath of life to their noses, for they are likenesses of Him which issued from His flesh. he shines in the sky for the benefit of their hearts; he has made herbs, cattle, and fish to nourish them. he has killed His enemies and destroyed His own children, because they had planned to make rebellion; He makes daylight for the benefit of their hearts, and he sails around in order to see them. he has raised up a shrine behind them, and when they weep, He hears. he has made them rulers even from the egg, a lifter to lift the load from the back of the weak man; He has made for them magic to be weapons to ward off what may happen.

Be watchful over it by night as by day. how has He killed the disaffected Even as a man strikes his son for his brother's sake, for God knows every name.

Do not be distressed at my utterance even when it gives laws concerning the king. Instruct yourself, that you may rise up as a man; then you will attain to my repute without anyone who accuses you. do not kill anyone who approaches you, but favor him, for God knows him. He who flourishes on earth is one of them, and they who serve the king are gods. Instill the love of you into all the world, for a good character is what is remembered... is perished, and it is said of you: "he who will destroy the time of suffering by those who are at the back in the House of Akhtoy, in praying for him who will come today.

See, I have told you the best of my inmost thoughts, which you should set steadfastly before your face.

The Leningrad Papyrus ends with a wordy colophon informing us that this particular copy was made by a scribe named Khamwese for his won use and that of his brother Mahu

The Teaching of King Ammenemes I to His Son Sesostris

Here begins the teaching which the late King of Upper and Lower Egypt, Sehetepibre, the son of Re Ammenemes made when he spoke in imparting truth to his son the Lord of All. He said: O you who appear as a god, here what I shall say to you, that you may be king of the land and rule the Banks, and achieve abundance of good fortune. Be on your guard against all who are subordinate to you when there occurs something to whose terrors no thought has been given; do not approach them in your solitude, trust no brother, know no friend, make no intimates, for there is no profit in it. When you go to rest, guard your own heart, for no man has partisans on the day of trouble. I gave to the poor man, I cherished the orphan, I caused him who had nothing to attain to wealth like him who was wealthy, but it was he who ate my bread who raised levies; he to whom I had given my hand created terror thereby; those who wore my fine linen looked on me as a shadow; and they who smeared on my myrrh poured water under me.

O you living images of me, my heirs among men, make for me a funeral oration which has not been heard before, a great deed of battle which has not been seen, for men fight in the arena and the past is forgotten; goodness cannot profit one who does not know him whom he should know. It was after supper, and night had fallen. I took an hour of recreation lying on my bed, for I was weary and I began to doze, when weapons were brandished and men agued about me. I acted like the snake of the desert, for I awoke at the fighting and was by myself, and I found that it was a combat with the guard. If I had made haste with weapons in my hand, I would have made the cowards retreat in confusion, but no one is brave at night, and no one can fight alone; no happy outcome can result without a protector. See, my injuries occurred while I was without you, before the entourage had heard that I was handing over to you, before I had sat down with you. Therefore I will give you good advice, because I neither fear them nor even think about them; I take no cognizance of the slackness of servants. Have women ever marshaled the ranks? Are brawlers nourished within a house? Are the waters opened up or the earthen banks destroyed? Are the citizens befooled because of what they have done?

Trouble has not come about me since I was born, and the like of my deeds through the exercise of my valor has not come to pass. I traveled to Elephantine, I turned back to the Delta; I have stood at the limits of the land and have seen its middle; I have attained the limits of my power by my strong arm and by my nature. It was I who made barley and loved grain; the Nile-god showed me respect in every open place, and none went hungry in my years, none went thirsty in them. Men dwelt in peace through what I had done, talking of me, for everything that I commanded was in good order. I have curbed lions, I have carried off crocodiles, I have crushed the people of Wawat, I have carried off the Medjay, I have made the Asiatics slink like gods. I have built for myself a house adorned with gold, its ceiling of lapis lazuli, its walls of silver, the doors of copper and the door-bolts of bronze, it having been made for eternity and prepared for everlasting. I know that the owner of it is the Lord of All. Indeed, many children are in the streets; the wise man agrees and the fool says "no," inasmuch as he who does not know it is devoid of vision. O my son Sesostris, may your legs walk; you are my own heart, and my eyes watch you. You were born in an hour of happiness in the presence of the sun-folk, and they give you praise. See, I have made a beginning and you have arranged the end. I have moored...what is in your heart... leaving the White Crown for the seed of the god. The fortification is in good order, beginning from....vessels are in the bark of Re. The kingship came into being in my presence, and there are none who could achieve my deeds of valor. Erect monuments, embellish your causeway, fight for... because he does not desire it in His Majesty's presence.

It has come happily to an end.

The Prophecies of Neferti

Now it so happened that when the late King Snefru was potent king in this entire land, one of these days it happened that the Council of the Residence entered into the Great House to give greeting, and when they had given greeting, they went out in accordance with their daily custom. Then said his Majesty to the seal-bearer who was at his side: Go and fetch for me the Council of the Residence which has gone out from here after having given greeting today. They were ushered in to him immediately, and again they prostrated themselves before His Majesty. And His Majesty said to them: Comrades, see, I have caused you to be summoned in order that you may seek out for me a son of yours who is wise, a brother of yours who is trustworthy, or a friend of yours who has achieved some noble deed, someone who shall say some fine words to me, choice phrases at the hearing of which My Majesty will be entertained. They prostrated themselves again before His Majesty: There is a Great Lector of Bastet, O Sovereign our lord, whose name is Neferti; he is a commoner valiant with his arm, he is a scribe skilled with his fingers, and he is a wealthy man who has more possessions than any of his equals. Let him be [permitted] to see Your Majesty. His Majesty said: Go and fetch him to me. And he was ushered in to him immediately.

He prostrated himself before His Majesty, and His Majesty said: Come, Neferti my friend, say some fine words to me, choice phrases at hearing which My Majesty will be entertained. The Lector Neferti said: Of what has happened or of what shall happen, O Sovereign, [my] lord? His Majesty said: Of what shall happen; today has come into being and one has passed it by. Thereupon he stretched out his hand to a box of writing material and took out a papyrus-roll and a palette, and he put into writing what the Lector Neferti said; he was a sage of the East who belonged to Bastet when she rises and he was a native of the Heliopolitan nome.

he brooded over what should happen in the land and considered the condition of the east, when the Asiatics raid and terrorize those at the harvest, taking away their teams engaged in plowing. He said: stir yourself, my hear, weep for this land in which you began, for he who is silent is a wrongdoer. See, that now exists which was spoken of as something dreadful. See, the great one is overthrown in the land in which you began. Do not become weary; see they are before your eyes; rise up against what is before you. See, there are great men in the governance of the land, yet what has been done is s though it had never been done. Re must begin by refounding the land, which is utterly ruined, and nothing remains; not even did a fingernail profit from what had been ordained. This land is destroyed and there are none who care for it; there are none who speak and there are none who act. Weeper, how fares this land? The sun is veiled, and will not shine when the people would see; none will live when the sun is veiled by cloud, and everyone is dulled by the lack of it.

I will speak of what is before my eyes, I will never foretell what is not to come. The river of Egypt is dry and men cross the water on foot; men will seek water for ships in order to navigate it, for their course has become the riverbank, and the bank serves for water; the place of water has become a riverbank, the south wind will oppose the north wind, and the sky will not be with one single wind. A strange bird will be born in the marshes of the Delta, and a nest shall be made for it on account of the neighbors, for men have caused it to approach through want. Perished are those erstwhile good things, the fish ponds of those who carry slit fish, teeming with fish and fowl. All good things have passed away, the land being cast away through trouble by means of that food of the Asiatics who pervade the land. Enemies have come into being in the east; Asiatics have come down into Egypt, for a fortress lacks another beside it, and no guard will hear. Men will hold back and look out by night, the fortress will be entered, and sleep will be banished from my eyes, so that I spend the night wakeful. Wild game will drink from the river of Egypt, taking their ease on their riverbanks through lack of anyone to fear. This land is in commotion, and no one knows what the result may be, for it is hidden from speech, sight, and hearing because of dullness, silence being to the fore.

I show you the land in calamity, for what had never happened has now happened. Men will take weapons of war and the land will live in confusion. Men will make arrows of bronze, men will beg for the bread of blood, men will laugh aloud at pain; none will weep at death, none will lie down hungry at death, and a man's heart will think of himself alone. None will dress hair today; hearts are entirely astray because of it, and a man sits quiet, turning his back, while one man kills another.

I show you a son as an enemy, a brother as a foe, a man killing his father. Every mouth is full of "Love me"; all good things have passed away; a law is decreed for the ruin of the land. Men wreak destruction on what has been made and make a desolation of what has been found; what has been made is as though it had never been made; a man's possessions are taken from him and are given to an outsider.

I show you the owner of but a little, while the outsider is content. He who did not fill for himself now goes empty; men give something unwillingly, so as to silence a talking mouth. A sentence is answered and a hand goes out with a stick; [men say]: "Do not kill him," but the discourse of speech is like fire to the heart, and none can endure utterance. The land is diminished, though its controllers are many; he who was rich in servants is despoiled and corn is trifling, even though the corn measure is great and it is measured to overflowing. Re separates himself from men; he shines, that the hour may be told, but no one knows when noon occurs, for no one can discern his shadow, no one is dazzled when [he] is seen; there are none whose eyes stream with water, for he is like the moon in the sky, though his accustomed time do [not] go astray, and his rays are in men's sight as on former occasions.

I show you the land in calamity; the weak-armed now possesses an arm, and men salute one who used to do the saluting. I show you [the lowermost] uppermost, men pursuing him who flees away; men are living in the necropolis. The poor man will achieve wealth, while the great lady will [beg] to exist; it is the poor who will eat bread, while servants are....; there will be no Heliopolitan nome to be the birth-land of every god.

A king of the South will come, Ameny by name, the son of a woman of Zety-land, a child of Khenkhen. He will assume the White Crown, he will wear the Red Crown, he will join together the Double Crown, he will propitiate the Two Lords with what they desire; the land will be enclosed in his grasp, the oars swinging, the people of his reign will rejoice, the well-born man will make his name forever and ever. Those who have fallen into evil and have planned rebellion have stultified their utterances through fear of him; the Asiatics will fall at the dread of him; the Libyans will fall at his flaming, the rebels at his wrath, the disaffected at the awe of him, while the uraeus which is on his forehead will pacify the disaffected. Men will build "Walls of the Ruler," and there will be no letting the Asiatics go down into Egypt that they may beg water after their accustomed fashion to let their herds drink. Right will come to its place again and Wrong will be thrust outside; joyful will be [he] who will see it and he who will serve the king. The learned man shall pour [a libation to me when he sees that what I have said] has come to pass.

It has come happily to an end.

The Admonitions of Ipuwer

It is impossible to give a date for the composition of this document. The surviving papyrus Papyrus Leiden 334 itself is a copy made during the New Kingdom. Ipuwer is generally supposed to have lived during the Middle Kingdom or the Second Intermediate Period, and the catastrophes he bewails to have taken place four centuries earlier during the First Intermediate Period.

Fringe historians often compare the contents of this papyrus with the second book of the bible, Exodus. Such comparisons between Egyptian texts and the bible are easily made and assuming Egyptian influence on the Hebrews is reasonable, given their at times close contacts. To conclude from these similarities that the Ipuwer Papyrus describes Egypt at the time of the Exodus requires a leap of faith not everybody is willing to make.

Lacunae in the papyrus text are marked by [...].

I

[..] The door [keepers] say: "Let us go and plunder."
The confectioners [...].
The washerman refuses to carry his load [...]
The bird [catchers] have drawn up in line of battle [... the inhabitants] of the Delta carry shields.
The brewers [...] sad.
A man regards his son as his enemy. Confusion [...] another.
Come and conquer; judge [...] what was ordained for you in the time of Horus, in the age [of the Ennead ...]. The virtuous man goes in mourning because of what has happened in the land [...] goes [...] the tribes of the desert have become Egyptians everywhere.
Indeed, the face is pale; [...] what the ancestors foretold has arrived at [fruition ...] the land is full of confederates, and a man goes to plough with his shield.
Indeed, the meek say: ["He who is ... of] face is as a well-born

man."

Indeed, [the face] is pale; the bowman is ready, wrongdoing is everywhere, and there is no man of yesterday.

Indeed, the plunderer [. . .] everywhere, and the servant takes what he finds.

Indeed, the Nile overflows, yet none plough for it[2]. Everyone says: "We do not know what will happen throughout the land."

Indeed, the women are barren and none conceive. Khnum fashions men no more because of the condition of the land.

II

Indeed, poor men have become owners of wealth, and he who could not make sandals for himself is now a possessor of riches.

Indeed, men's slaves, their hearts are sad, and magistrates do not fraternize with their people when they shout.

Indeed, [hearts] are violent, pestilence is throughout the land, blood is everywhere, death is not lacking, and the mummy-cloth speaks even before one comes near it.

Indeed, many dead are buried in the river; the stream is a sepulcher and the place of embalmment has become a stream.

Indeed, noblemen are in distress, while the poor man is full of joy. Every town says: "Let us suppress the powerful among us."[3]

Indeed, men are like ibises. Squalor is throughout the land, and there are none indeed whose clothes are white in these times.

Indeed, the land turns around as does a potter's wheel; the robber is a possessor of riches and [the rich man is become] a plunderer.

Indeed, trusty servants are [. . .]; the poor man [complains]: "How

---

[2] the Nile overflows, yet none plough for it: The collapse of the Old Kingdom civilisation is generally attributed to a repeated failure of the Nile to inundate the flood plain. A few consecutive crop failures can result in many subsequent years of suffering, as all the grain that can be grown and which is to serve as seed, will been consumed as food.

[3] Let us suppress the powerful among us: Let us banish many from us John A.Wilson

terrible! What am I to do?"
Indeed, the river is blood, yet men drink of it. Men shrink from human beings and thirst after water.[4]
Indeed, gates, columns and walls are burnt up[5], while the hall of the palace stands firm and endures.
Indeed, the ship of [the southerners] has broken up; towns are destroyed and Upper Egypt has become an empty waste.
Indeed, crocodiles [are glutted] with the fish they have taken, for men go to them of their own accord[6]; it is the destruction of the land. Men say: "Do not walk here; behold, it is a net." Behold, men tread [the water] like fishes, and the frightened man cannot distinguish it because of terror.
Indeed, men are few, and he who places his brother in the ground is everywhere. When the wise man speaks, [he flees without delay].
Indeed, the well-born man [...] through lack of recognition, and the child of his lady has become the son of his maidservant.

III

Indeed, the desert is throughout the land, the nomes are laid waste, and barbarians [7]from abroad have come to Egypt[8].

---

[4] Indeed, the river is blood, yet men drink of it. Men shrink from human beings and thirst after water: Why really, the River is blood. If one drinks of it, one rejects it as human and thirsts for water. Wilson

[5] gates, columns and walls are burnt up: doors, columns, and floor planks are burned up Wilson

[6] crocodiles [are glutted] with the fish they have taken, for men go to them of their own accord: crocodiles [sink] down because of what they have carried off, for men go to them of their own accord. Wilson

[7] barbarians : Egyptians saw themselves as the pinnacle of creation: their land was The Land, their people were The People. In this their attitude was similar to that of other ancient and not so ancient peoples.

[8] from abroad have come to Egypt: Times of weak central power opened opportunities for foreigners to infiltrate the country in even larger numbers than ordinarily: The Nubian Medjay during the First Intermediate Period, the Hyksos during the Second. Still, they probably numbered in the thousands rather in the hundred thousands.

Indeed, men arrive [...] and indeed, there are no Egyptians[9] anywhere.

Indeed, gold and lapis lazuli, silver and turquoise, carnelian and amethyst, Ibhet-stone and [...] are strung on the necks of maidservants. Good things are throughout the land, yet housewives say: "Oh that we had something to eat!"

Indeed, [...] noblewomen. Their bodies are in sad plight by reason of their rags, and their hearts sink when greeting [one another]. Indeed, chests of ebony are broken up, and precious ssndm-wood is cleft asunder in beds [...].

Indeed, the builders [of pyramids have become] cultivators, and those who were in the sacred bark are now yoked [to it]. None shall indeed sail northward to Byblos today; what shall we do for cedar trees for our mummies, and with the produce of which priests are buried and with the oil of which [chiefs] are embalmed as far as Keftiu? They come no more; gold is lacking [...] and materials for every kind of craft have come to an end. The [...] of the palace is despoiled. How often do people of the oases come with their festival spices, mats, and skins, with fresh rdmt-plants, grease of birds ... ?

Indeed, Elephantine and Thinis [...] of Upper Egypt, but without paying taxes owing to civil strife. Lacking are grain, charcoal, irtyw-fruit, m'w-wood, nwt-wood, and brushwood. The work of craftsmen and [...] are the profit of the palace. To what purpose is a treasury without its revenues? Happy indeed is the heart of the king when truth comes to him! And every foreign land [comes]! That is our fate and that is our happiness! What can we do about it? All is ruin!

Indeed, laughter is perished and is [no longer] made; it is groaning that is throughout the land, mingled with complaints.

---

[9] Egyptians: people Wilson cf.

IV

Indeed, every dead person is as a well-born man. Those who were Egyptians [have become] foreigners and are thrust aside.
Indeed, hair [has fallen out] for everybody, and the man of rank can no longer be distinguished from him who is nobody.
Indeed, [. . .] because of noise; noise is not [. . .] in years of noise, and there is no end [of] noise.
Indeed, great and small [say]: "I wish I might die." Little children say: "He should not have caused [me] to live."
Indeed, the children of princes are dashed against walls, and the children of the neck[10] are laid out on the high ground[11].
Indeed, those who were in the place of embalmment are laid out on the high ground, and the secrets of the embalmers are thrown down because of it.
Indeed, that has perished which yesterday was seen, and the land is left over to its weakness like the cutting of flax.
Indeed, the Delta in its entirety will not be hidden, and Lower Egypt puts trust in trodden roads. What can one do? No [. . .] exist anywhere, and men say: "Perdition to the secret place!"
Behold, it is in the hands of those who do not know it like those who know it. The desert dwellers are skilled in the crafts[12] of the Delta.
Indeed, citizens are put to the corn-rubbers, and those who used to don fine linen are beaten with . . . Those who used never to see the day have gone out unhindered; those who were on their husbands' beds, let them lie on rafts. I say: "It is too heavy for me," concerning rafts bearing myrrh. Load them with vessels filled with [. . . Let] them know the palanquin. As for the butler, he is ruined. There are no remedies for it; noblewomen suffer like maidservants, minstrels are at the looms within the weaving-rooms, and what they sing to the Songstress-goddess is mourning.

---

[10] ...the children of the neck i.e. holding onto the neck of the carrying grown-up: The once prayed-for children Wilson
[11] on the high ground: burial ground above the flood plain.
[12] crafts: work Wilson

Talkers [. . .] corn-rubbers.
Indeed, all female slaves are free with their tongues, and when their mistress speaks, it is irksome to the maidservants.
Indeed, trees are felled and branches are stripped off[13].

V

I have separated him and his household slaves, and men will say when they hear it: "Cakes are lacking for most children; there is no food [. . .]. What is the taste of it like today?"
Indeed, magnates are hungry and perishing, followers are followed [. . .] because of complaints.
Indeed, the hot-tempered man says: "If I knew where God is, then I would serve Him."
Indeed, [Right] pervades the land in name, but what men do in trusting to it is Wrong.
Indeed, runners are fighting over the spoil [of] the robber, and all his property is carried off.
Indeed, all animals, their hearts weep; cattle moan because of the state of the land.
Indeed, the children of princes are dashed against walls, and the children of the neck are laid out on the high ground. Khnum groans because of his weariness.
Indeed, terror kills; the frightened man opposes what is done against your enemies. Moreover, the few are pleased, while the rest are . . . Is it by following the crocodile and cleaving it asunder? Is it by slaying the lion roasted on the fire? [Is it] by sprinkling for Ptah and taking [. . .]? Why do you give to him? There is no reaching him. It is misery which you give to him.
Indeed, slaves . . . throughout the land, and the strong man sends to everyone; a man strikes his maternal brother. What is it that has been done? I speak to a ruined man.

---

[13] trees are felled and branches are stripped off: the wholesale destruction of trees causes serious fuel problems, as witnessed nowadays in the Sahel region of sub-saharan Africa

Indeed, the ways are [. . .], the roads are watched[14]; men sit in the bushes until the benighted traveler comes in order to plunder his burden, and what is upon him is taken away. He is belabored with blows of a stick and murdered.
Indeed, that has perished which yesterday was seen, and the land is left over to its weakness like the cutting of flax, commoners coming and going in dissolution [. . .].

VI

Would that there were an end of men, without conception, without birth! Then would the land be quiet from noise and tumult be no more.
Indeed, [men eat] herbage and wash [it] down with water; neither fruit nor herbage can be found [for] the birds, and [. . .] is taken away from the mouth of the pig. No face is bright which you have [. . .] for me through hunger.
Indeed, everywhere barley has perished and men are stripped of clothes, spice, and oil; everyone says: "There is none." The storehouse is empty and its keeper is stretched on the ground; a happy state of affairs! . . .
Would that I had raised my voice at that moment, that it might have saved me from the pain in which I am.
Indeed, the private council-chamber, its writings are taken away and the mysteries which were [in it] are laid bare[15].
Indeed, magic spells are divulged[16]; smw- and shnw-spells[17] are frustrated because they are remembered by men.
Indeed, public offices are opened and their inventories are taken

---

[14] the ways are [. . .], the roads are watched: the ways [are not] guarded roads Wilson

[15] the private council-chamber, its writings are taken away and the mysteries which were [in it] are laid bare the writings of the augurs enclosure are read. The place of secrets which was so formerly is now laid bare Wilson

[16] magic spells are divulged: Magic has always shunned the light of day and becomes ineffectual when scrutinized with a critical mind. Strangely, this has never prevented people from believing in it.

[17] smw- and shnw spells: Go-spells and Enfold-spells Wilson

away; the serf has become an owner of serfs.

Indeed, [scribes] are killed and their writings are taken away. Woe is me because of the misery of this time!

Indeed, the writings of the scribes of the cadaster are destroyed, and the corn of Egypt is common property[18].

Indeed, the laws of the council chamber are thrown out; indeed, men walk on them in public places, and poor men break them up in the streets.

Indeed, the poor man has attained to the state of the Nine Gods, and the erstwhile procedure of the House of the Thirty[19] is divulged.

Indeed, the great council-chamber is a popular resort, and poor men come and go to the Great Mansions.

Indeed, the children of magnates are ejected into the streets; the wise man agrees and the fool says "no," and it is pleasing in the sight of him who knows nothing about it.

Indeed, those who were in the place of embalmment are laid out on the high ground, and the secrets of the embalmers are thrown down because of it.

VII

Behold, the fire has gone up on high, and its burning goes forth against the enemies of the land.

Behold, things have been done which have not happened for a long time past; the king has been deposed by the rabble.

Behold, he who was buried as a falcon[20] [is devoid] of biers, and what the pyramid concealed has become empty.

Behold, it has befallen that the land has been deprived of the

---

[18] the corn of Egypt is common property: The grain-sustenance of Egypt is now a come-and-get-it. Wilson The storage of surplus grain and its redistribution was one of the corner stones of the Egyptian economy.

[19] House of Thirty: Tribunal, cf. Hail Eater of entrails who came forth from the House of Thirty, I have not committed perjury. from the Book of the Dead transl. by Allen and Faulkner

[20] Falcon: the pharaoh, son of Horus

kingship by a few lawless men.

Behold, men have fallen into rebellion against the Uraeus, the [. . .] of Re, even she who makes the Two Lands content.

Behold, the secret of the land whose limits were unknown is divulged, and the Residence is thrown down in a moment.

Behold, Egypt is fallen to pouring of water, and he who poured water on the ground has carried off the strong man in misery.

Behold, the Serpent is taken from its hole, and the secrets of the Kings of Upper and Lower Egypt are divulged.

Behold, the Residence is afraid because of want, and [men go about] unopposed to stir up strife.

Behold, the land has knotted itself up with confederacies, and the coward takes the brave man's property.

Behold, the Serpent[21] [. . .] the dead: he who could not make a sarcophagus for himself is now the possessor of a tomb.

Behold, the possessors of tombs are ejected on to the high ground, while he who could not make a coffin for himself is now [the possessor] of a treasury.

Behold, this has happened [to] men; he who could not build a room for himself is now a possessor of walls.

Behold, the magistrates of the land are driven out throughout the land: [. . .] are driven out from the palaces.

Behold, noble ladies are now on rafts, and magnates are in the labor establishment, while he who could not sleep even on walls is now the possessor of a bed[22].

Behold, the possessor of wealth now spends the night thirsty, while he who once begged his dregs for himself is now the possessor of overflowing bowls.

Behold, the possessors of robes are now in rags, while he who could not weave for himself is now a possessor of fine linen.

---

[21] Serpent: guardian-serpent Wilson

[22] Behold, noble ladies are now on rafts, and magnates are in the labor establishment, while he who could not sleep even on walls is now the possessor of a bed. Behold, nobles' ladies are now gleaners, and nobles are in the workhouse. But he who never even slept on a plank is now the owner of a bed. Wilson

Behold, he who could not build a boat for himself is now the possessor of a fleet; their erstwhile owner looks at them, but they are not his.

Behold, he who had no shade is now the possessor of shade, while the erstwhile possessors of shade are now in the full blast of the storm.

Behold, he who was ignorant of the lyre is now the possessor of a harp, while he who never sang for himself now vaunts the Songstress-goddess[23].

Behold, those who possessed vessel-stands of copper [. . .] not one of the jars thereof has been adorned.

VIII

Behold, he who slept wifeless through want [finds] riches, while he whom he never saw stands making dole.

Behold, he who had no property is now a possessor of wealth, and the magnate praises him.

Behold, the poor of the land have become rich, and the [erstwhile owner] of property is one who has nothing.

Behold, serving-men have become masters of butlers, and he who was once a messenger now sends someone else.

Behold, he who had no loaf is now the owner of a barn, and his storehouse is provided with the goods of another.

Behold, he whose hair is fallen out and who had no oil has now become the possessors of jars of sweet myrrh.

Behold, she who had no box is now the owner of a coffer, and she who had to look at her face in the water is now the owner of a mirror.

Behold, [. . .].

Behold, a man is happy eating his food. Consume your goods in gladness and unhindered, for it is good for a man to eat his food; God commands it for him whom He has favored [. . .].

[Behold, he who did not know] his god now offers to him with

---

[23] Songstress-goddess: goddess of music Wilson

incense of another [who is] not known [to him].
[Behold,] great ladies, once possessors of riches, now give their children for beds.
Behold, a man [to whom is given] a noble lady as wife, her father protects him, and he who has not [. . .] killing him.
Behold, the children of magistrates are [. . . the calves] of cattle [are given over] to the plunderers.
Behold, priests transgress with the cattle of the poor [. . .].
Behold, he who could not slaughter for himself now slaughters bulls, and he who did not know how to carve now sees [. . .].
Behold, priests transgress with geese, which are given [to] the gods instead of oxen.
Behold, maidservants [. . .] offer ducks; noblewomen [. . .].
Behold, noblewomen flee; the overseers of [. . .] and their [children] are cast down through fear of death.
[Behold,] the chiefs of the land flee; there is no purpose for them because of want. The lord of [. . .].

IX

[Behold,] those who once owned beds are now on the ground, while he who once slept in squalor now lays out a skin-mat for himself.
Behold, noblewomen go hungry, while the priests[24] are sated with what has been prepared for them.
Behold, no offices are in their right place, like a herd running at random without a herdsman.
Behold, cattle stray and there is none to collect them, but everyone fetches for himself those that are branded with his name[25].
Behold, a man is slain beside his brother, who runs away and abandons him to save his own skin.

---

[24] priests: king's men Wilson
[25] everyone fetches for himself those that are branded with his name: Every man takes for himself and brands them with his name. Wilson

Behold, he who had no yoke of oxen is now the owner of a herd, and he who could find for himself no ploughman is now the owner of cattle.
Behold, he who had no grain is now the owner of granaries, and he who had to fetch loan-corn for himself is now one who issues it.
Behold, he who had no dependents is now an owner of serfs, and he who was [a magnate] now performs his own errands.
Behold, the strong men of the land, the condition of the people is not reported [to them]. All is ruin!
Behold, no craftsmen work, for the enemies of the land have impoverished its craftsmen.
[Behold, he who once recorded] the harvest now knows nothing about it, while he who never ploughed [for himself is now the owner of corn; the reaping] takes place but is not reported. The scribe [sits in his office], but his hands [are idle] in it.
Destroyed is [. . .] in that time, and a man looks [on his friend as] an adversary. The infirm man brings coolness [to what is hot . . .] fear [. . . . . .]. Poor men [. . . the land] is not bright because of it.

X

Destroyed is [. . .] their food is taken from them [. . . through] fear of his terror. The commoner begs [. . .] messenger, but not [. . .] time. He is captured laden with goods and [all his property] is taken away. [. . .] men pass by his door [. . .] the outside of the wall, a shed, and rooms containing falcons. It is the common man who will be vigilant, the day having dawned on him without his dreading it. Men run because of [. . . for] the temple of the head, strained through a woven cloth within the house. What they make are tents, just like the desert folk.
Destroyed is the doing of that for which men are sent by retainers in the service of their masters; they have no readiness.
Behold, they are five men, and they say: "Go on the road you know, for we have arrived."
Lower Egypt weeps; the king's storehouse is the common

property of everyone, and the entire palace is without its revenues. To it belong emmer and barley, fowl and fish; to it belong white cloth and fine linen, copper and oil; to it belong carpet and mat, [...] flowers and wheat-sheaf and all good revenues ... If the ... it in the palace were delayed, men would be devoid [of ...].
Destroy the enemies of the august Residence, splendid of magistrates [...] in it like [...]; indeed, the Governor of the City goes unescorted.
Destroy [the enemies of the august Residence,] splendid [...].
[Destroy the enemies of] that erstwhile august Residence, manifold of laws [...]. [Destroy the enemies of] that erstwhile august [Residence ...].
Destroy the enemies of that erstwhile august Residence [...] none can stand [...].
Destroy the enemies of that erstwhile august Residence, manifold of offices; indeed [...].
Remember to immerse [...] him who is in pain when he is sick in his body; show respect [...] because of his god that he may guard the utterance [...] his children who are witnesses of the surging of the flood.

XI

Remember[26] to [......]... shrine, to fumigate with incense and to offer water in a jar in the early morning.
Remember [to bring] fat r-geese, trp-geese, and ducks[27] and to offer god's offerings to the gods.
Remember to chew natron[28] and to prepare white bread; a man [should do it] on the day of wetting the head.

---

[26] Remember: The things to remember are the duties of the priests, first among them the pharaoh as High Priest, to their gods. In accordance with the magical thinking of the day and which still persists among many believers the meticulous fulfilment of duties brings with it the favour of the gods and thus the well-being of the pious.

[27] ducks: sat-geese Wilson

[28] natron: used for cleaning teeth, cf.

Remember to erect flagstaffs and to carve offering stones, the priest cleansing the chapels and the temple being plastered white like milk; to make pleasant the odor of the horizon and to provide bread-offerings.
Remember to observe regulations, to fix dates correctly, and to remove him who enters on the priestly office in impurity of body, for that is doing it wrongfully, it is destruction of the heart [...] the day which precedes eternity, the months [...] years are known.
Remember to slaughter oxen [...].
Remember to go forth purged [...] who calls to you; to put r-geese on the fire [...] to open the jar [...] the shore of the waters [...] of women [...] clothing [... ...] to give praise ... in order to appease you.
[...] lack of people; come [...] Re who commands [...] worshipping him [...] West until [...] are diminished [...]. Behold, why does he seek to fashion [men ...]? The frightened man is not distinguished from the violent one.

XII

He brings coolness upon heat; men say: "He is the herdsman of mankind, and there is no evil in his heart." Though his herds are few, yet he spends a day to collect them, their hearts being on fire.
Would that he had perceived their nature in the first generation; then he would have imposed obstacles, he would have stretched out his arm against them, he would have destroyed their herds[29] and their heritage. Men desire the giving of birth, but sadness supervenes, with needy people on all sides. So it is, and it will not pass away while the gods who are in the midst of it exist. Seed goes forth into mortal women, but none are found on the road.
Combat has gone forth, and he who should be a redresser of evils

---

[29] their herds: the seed thereof Wilson

is one who commits them; neither do men act as pilot in their hour of duty. Where is he today? Is he asleep? Behold, his power is not seen.

If we had been fed, I would not have found you, I would not have been summoned in vain; "Aggression against it means pain of heart" is a saying on the lips of everyone. Today he who is afraid . . . a myriad of people; [. . .] did not see [. . .] against the enemies of [. . .] at his outer chamber; who enter the temple [. . .] weeping for him [. . .] that one who confounds what he has said . . . The land has not fallen [. . .] the statues are burned and their tombs destroyed [. . .] he sees the day of [. . .]. He who could not make for himself [. . .] between sky and ground is afraid of everybody. . . . if he does it . . . what you dislike taking.

Authority, knowledge, and truth are with you, yet confusion is what you set throughout the land, also the noise of tumult. Behold, one deals harm to another, for men conform to what you have commanded. If three men travel on the road, they are found to be only two, for the many kill the few.

XIII

Does a herdsman desire death? Then may you command reply to be made, because it means that one loves, another detests; it means that their existences are few everywhere; it means that you have acted so as to bring those things to pass. You have told lies, and the land is a weed which destroys men, and none can count on life. All these years are strife, and a man is murdered on his housetop even though he was vigilant in his gate lodge. Is he brave and saves himself? It means he will live.

When men send a servant for humble folk, he goes on the road until he sees the flood; the road is washed out and he stands worried. What is on him is taken away, he is belabored with blows of a stick and wrongfully slain. Oh that you could taste a little of the misery of it! Then you would say [. . .] from someone else as a wall, over and above [. . .] hot . . . years . . . [. . .].

[It is indeed good] when ships fare upstream [. . . . . .] robbing them.

It is indeed good [...]. [It is indeed] good when the net is drawn in and birds are tied up [...].

It is [indeed] good [...] dignities for them, and the roads are passable.

It is indeed good when the hands of men build pyramids, when ponds are dug and plantations of the trees of the gods are made.

It is indeed good when men are drunk; they drink myt and their hearts are happy.

XIV

It is indeed good when shouting is in men's mouths, when the magnates of districts stand looking on at the shouting in their houses, clad in a cloak, cleansed in front and well-provided within[30].

It is indeed good when beds are prepared and the headrests of magistrates are safely secured. Every man's need is satisfied with a couch in the shade, and a door is now shut on him who once slept in the bushes.

It is indeed good when fine linen is spread out on New Year's Day [...] on the bank; when fine linen is spread out and cloaks are on the ground. The overseer of [...] the trees, the poor [... ...] in their midst like Asiatics [...]. Men [...] the state thereof; they have come to an end of themselves; none can be found to stand up and protect themselves [...].

Everyone fights for his sister and saves his own skin. Is it Nubians? Then will we guard ourselves; warriors are made many in order to ward off foreigners. Is it Libyans? Then we will turn away. The Medjay are pleased with Egypt[31].

---

[30] well-provided within: firm-bellied Wilson

[31] The Medjay are pleased with Egypt: The Madjoi fortunately are with Egypt. Wilson; The Medjai are content with Egypt." Lichtheim

XV

How comes it that every man kills his brother? The troops whom we marshaled for ourselves have turned into foreigners and have taken to ravaging[32]. What has come to pass through it is informing the Asiatics of the state of the land; all the desert folk are possessed with the fear of it. What the plebs have tasted [. . .] without giving Egypt over [to] the sand. It is strong [. . .] speak about you after years [. . .] devastate itself, it is the threshing floor which nourishes their houses [. . .] to nourish his children [. . .] said by the troops [. . . . . .] fish [. . .] gum, lotus leaves [. . .] excess of food.

XVI

What Ipuwer said when he addressed the Majesty of the Lord of All: [. . .] all herds. It means that ignorance of it is what is pleasing to the heart. You have done what was good in their hearts and you have nourished the people with it. They cover their faces through fear of the morrow.
That is how a man grows old before he dies, while his son is a lad of understanding; he does not open [his] mouth to speak to you, but you seize him in the doom of death [. . .] weep [. . .] go [. . .] after you, that the land may be [. . .] on every side.

XVII

If men call to [. . .] weep [. . .] them, who break into the tombs and burn the statues [. . .] the corpses of the nobles [. . . . . .] of directing work.

---

[32] foreigners and have taken to ravaging: barbarians, beginning to destroy that from which they took their being Wilson

The Tale of The Eloquent Peasant

There was a man, Hunanup by name, a peasant of Sechet-hemat, and he had a wife,......by name. Then said this peasant to his wife: "Behold, I am going down to Egypt to bring back bread for my children. Go in and measure the grain that we still have in our storehouse,............bushel." Then he measured for her eight bushels of grain. Then this peasant said to his wife: "Behold, two bushels of grain shall be left for bread for you and the children. But make for me the six bushels into bread and beer for each of the days that I shall be on the road." Then this peasant went down to Egypt after he had loaded his asses with all the good produce of Sechet-hemat.

This peasant set out and journeyed southward to Ehnas. He came to a point opposite Per-fefi, north of Medenit, and found there a man standing on the bank, Dehuti-necht by name, who was the son of a man named Iseri, who was one of the serfs of the chief steward, Meruitensi.

Then said this Dehuti-necht, when he saw the asses of this peasant which appealed to his covetousness: "Oh that some good god would help me to rob this peasant of his goods!"

The house of Dehuti-necht stood close to the side of the path, which was narrow, not wide. It was about the width of a ....-cloth, and upon one side of it was the water and upon the other side was growing grain. Then said Dehitu-necht to his servant: "Hasten and bring me a shawl from the house!" And it was brought at once. Then he spread this shawl upon the middle of the road, and it extended, one edge to the water, and the other to the grain.

The peasant came along the path which was the common highway. Then said Dehuti-necht: "Look out, peasant, do not trample on my clothes!" The peasant answered: "I will do as you wish; I will go in the right way!" As he was turning to the upper side, Dehuti-necht said: "Does my grain serve you as a road?" Then said the peasant: "I am going in the right way. The bank is steep and the path lies near the grain and you have stopped up the road ahead with your clothes. Will you, then, not let me go by?" Upon that one of the asses took a mouthful of grain. Then said Dehuti-necht: "See, I Will take away your ass because it has eaten my grain."

Then the peasant said: "I am going in the right way. As one side was made mpassable I have led my ass along the other, and will you seize it because it has taken a mouthful of grain? But I know the lord of this property; it belongs to the chief steward, Meruitensi. It is he who punishes every robber in this whole land. Shall I, then, be robbed in his domain?"

Then said Dehuti-necht: "Is it not a proverb which the people employ: The name of the poor is only known on account of his lord?' It is I who speak to you, but the chief steward of whom you think." Then he took a rod from a green tamarisk and beat all his limbs with it, and seized his asses and drove them into his compound.

Thereupon the peasant wept loudly on account of the pain of what had been done to him. Dehuti-necht said to him: "Don't cry so loud, peasant, or you shall go to the city of the dead." The peasant said: "You beat me and steal my goods, and will you also take the wail away from my mouth? O Silence-maker! Give me my goods again! May I never cease to cry out, if you fear!"

The peasant consumed four days, during which he besought Dehuti-necht, but he did not grant him his rights. Then this peasant went to the south, to Ehnas to implore the chief steward, Meruitensi. He met him as he was coming out of the canal-door of his compound to embark in his boat. Thereupon the peasant said: "Oh let me lay before you this affair. Permit one of your trusted servants to come to me, that I may send him to you concerning it." Then the steward Meruitensi, sent one of his servants to him, and he sent back by him an account of the whole affair. Then the chief steward, Meruitensi, laid the case of Dehuti-necht before his attendant officials, and they said to him: "Lord, it is presumably a case of one of your peasants who has gone against another peasant near him. Behold, it is customary with peasants to so conduct themselves toward others who are near them. Shall we beat Dehuti-necht for a little natron and a little salt? Command him to restore it and he will restore it."

The chief steward, Meruitensi, remained silent---he answered neither the officials nor the peasant. The peasant then came to entreat the chief steward Meruitensi, for the first time, and said: "Chief steward, my lord, you are greatest of the great, you are guide of all that which is not and which is. When you embark on the sea of truth, that you may go sailing upon it, then shall not the.........strip away your sail, then your ship shall not remain fast, then shall no misfortune happen to your mast then shall your spars not be broken, then shall you not be stranded---if you run fast aground, the waves shall not break upon you, then you shall not taste the impurities of the river, then you shall not behold the face of fear, the shy fish shall come to you, and you shall capture the fat birds. For you are the father of the orphan, the husband of the widow, the brother of the desolate, the garment of the motherless. Let me place your name in this land higher than all good laws: you guide without avarice, you great one free from meanness, who destroys deceit, who creates truthfulness. Throw the evil to the ground. I will speak hear me. Do justice, O you praised one, whom the praised ones praise. Remove my oppression: behold, I have a heavy weight to carry; behold, I am troubled of soul; examine me, I am in sorrow."[33]

This peasant came to implore him for the eighth time, and said: "Chief steward, my lord, man falls on account of............ Greed is absent from a good merchant. His good commerce is......... Your heart is greedy, it does not become you. You despoil: this is not praiseworthy for you.........Your daily rations are in your house; your body is well filled. The officers, who are set as a protection against injustice,---a curse to the shameless are these officers, who are set as a bulwark against lies. Fear of you has not

---

[33] *Barton: Meruitensi is so pleased with the eloquence of the peasant that he passed him on to another officer and he to still another until he came before the king. Altogether the peasant made nine addresses. His eighth address follows.*

deterred me from supplicating you; if you think so, you have not known my heart. The Silent one, who turns to report to you his difficulties, is not afraid to present them to you. Your real estate is in the country, your bread is on your estate, your food is in the storehouse. Your officials give to you and you take it. Are you, then, not a robber? They plow for you.......... for you to the plots of arable land. Do the truth for the sake of the Lord of Truth. You reed of a scribe, you roll of a book, you palette, you god Thoth, you ought to keep yourself far removed from injustice. You virtuous one, you should be virtuous, you virtuous one, you should be really virtuous. Further, truth is true to eternity. She goes with those who perform her to the region of the dead. He will be laid in the coffin and committed to the earth; ---his name will not perish from the earth, but men will remember him on account of his property: so runs the right interpretation of the divine word.

"Does it then happen that the scales stand aslant? Or is it thinkable that the scales incline to one side? Behold, if I come not, if another comes, then you host opportunity to speak as one who answers, as one who addresses the silent, as one who responds to him who has not spoken to you. You have not been..........; You have not been sick. You have not fled, you have not departed. But you have not yet granted me any reply to this beautiful word which comes from the mouth of the sun-god himself: Speak the truth; do the truth: for it is great, it is mighty, it is everlasting. It will obtain for you merit, and will lead you to veneration.' For does the scale stand aslant? It is their scale-pans that bear the objects, and in just scales there is no.............. wanting."[34]

Then the chief steward, Meruitensi, sent two servants to bring him back. Thereupon the peasant feared that he would suffer thirst, as a punishment imposed upon him for what he had said. Then the peasant said.............

Then said the chief steward, Meruitensi: "Fear not, peasant! See, you shall remain with me."

---

[34] *Barton: After a ninth speech on the part of the peasant, the tale concludes as follows.*

Then said the peasant: "I live because I eat of your bread and drink your beer forever."

Then said the chief steward, Meruitensi: "Come out here............" Then he caused them to bring, written on a new roll, all the addresses of these days. The chief steward sent them to his majesty, the king of Upper and Lower Egypt, Neb-kau-re, the blessed, and they were more agreeable to the heart of his majesty than all that was in his land. His majesty said, "Pass sentence yourself my beloved son!" Then the chief steward, Meruitensi, caused two servants to go and bring a list of the household of Dehuti-necht from the government office, and his possessions were six persons, with a selection from his.........., from his barley, from his spelt, from his asses, from his swine, from his..........[35]

---

[35] *Barton: From this point on only a few words of the tale can be made out, but it appears from these that the goods selected from the estate of Dehuti-necht were given to the peasant and he was sent home rejoicing.*

www.ingramcontent.com/pod-product-compliance
Lightning Source LLC
Chambersburg PA
CBHW060502110426
42738CB00055B/2593